The Under Side of Snow

Poems by LoVerne Brown

ISBN 0-938711-41-5

Library of Congress Cataloging Number 96-60890

Tecolote Publications
San Diego, California

Printed in the United States of America.

This book is lovingly dedicated
to
four very young people
whose footsteps in the sands of time
will be found mostly in
the twenty-first century:

Justin Daniel Csencsits
Garret Anderson Csencsits
Jeremy Aaron Cumbey
Joseph Winston Kenneth Leonard

Contents

The Under Side of Snow

The Under Side of Snow

It was always a surprise to the children
how quickly the spring and summer changed places
one morning snow so deep
the school bus could not run
next day so warm icicles from the eaves
loosened and fell into the peony bushes,
then snow again and a chill wind
howling in the chimney.

It was on that night of wind
that their father brought in twin lambs
wrapped in a horse blanket
wet and shivering
smelling mysteriously of blood and birth,
then out of strips of flannel fashioned milksops,
dipped them in milk and thrust one in each mouth,
sat stoking fire and lambs until the sun rose.

The children when they wakened squealed delight
to see their lambs upright on determined legs
willing to endure caresses for a full minute
before bleating a preference for their mother.

Then came a morning spring returned to stay.
In the creek below the apple orchard
ice like broken sheets of window glass
elbowed its way to river,
and the children
exploring the under side of snow
found arbutus in bud
red berries of wintergreen
beside them a frozen sparrow.
Life and death together,
as they always travel....

As the children, climbing the hill,
found their lambs again—
one dead and sadly flattened against the earth,
one at the mother's flank,
avidly appraising
her plenitude of milksops—
all his for the taking!

Sun on a Sunday

It is summer—almost August—hot all the time
The morning paper, delivered an hour ago,
is already parboiled.
My window faces east,
when I open the blinds
I find a malingering sun
who surely by now should be warming
whales in the ocean,
still lolling unashamed on my areaway,
insolent elbow at rest on my window sill,
his red hot gaze intent on my philodendron.

I close him out,
walk barefoot into my kitchen,
where the cool floor blesses my soles,
open the refrigerator,
let cold air billow about me.

A peach on a platter
startles a memory
of long ago cutting sheds
in the central valley
where, as I sliced fruit
for the drying trays,
fuzz crawled live as spiders
from wrist to armpit.

The peach is not aggressive.
Fuzz carefully wiped away,
skin cold and ruddy
amenable to the knife.
When I cut it open
the garnet stone falls free
its rosy flesh slides fragrantly
into a bowl.

4

I forgive the laggard sun
as I linger with peach and paper.
In summer, on Sunday morning,
the best way to use time is not to.

After the Verdict
(October 6, 1995)

The worst punishment is not to be punished.
Life in prison would have been pleasant enough—
even death's row would have its compensations,
flowers, cards, protestations of love,
would people the cell,
money would accrue
while you waited for a governor
to pardon you...
Now life will be your jailer
and life is without mercy.
Remembered eyes will study you
from a younger face,
spring rain on the roof
will be like blood
dripping on pavement,
your golf club will burden your hand
like the weight of that knife,
and a woman's body—
no matter how much you pay her—
will be like a glove
you can never quite fit into.

The Rapist's Child

The moon had never looked so arrogant
or so uncaring as on that November night
when Melita, 15, crouched by the alley dumpster
to birth the rapist's child.
                                        It slid easily
out of her, lay inert on her spread-out jacket,
a boy, shiny as a fish, not breathing, not alive.
This did not surprise her. She had felt his death
within her two days before—a rough spasm
as if he fought it, then quiet, and a coldness
spreading along her limbs.
                                        She looked at him
for clues to her attacker, whose face she had never
seen. Closed eyes and puckered mouth
retained their secret. She pulled her jacket round him,
wrapped it into a bundle, tied her belt
about it, thrust bundle into bag,
bag into dumpster, then walked unsteadily
back to the house.
                                        She saw no lights were lit.
No one had marked her going. She had left open
the garage door. There, in the little shower
where her father changed after work, she cleansed herself,
wrapped the debris of birth in her soiled clothes,
put the whole packet on the smoldering coals
of the stoked furnace; then, naked and shivering,
toiled up the stairs to bed.
                                        Lying long awake,
she watched the moonlight move on a flowered path
across the wall paper, thought of the plans she'd made,
had the boy lived, to clothe him in a nightshirt
stolen from her sister's baby and carry him
in a grocery box to the porch of the two nurses
who lived in the next block. Well, this was better.
She slept. Next morning, she dressed and went to school.

And nothing happened. Her family noticed nothing,
her friends and teachers nothing. The second morning
she heard the clank of the dumpster being emptied.
The baby went with the garbage into a landfill
and was never found. In time her memory
walled it all away as if it had never happened.
She finished school, got a job and married Allen.
No remembrance of violence shadowed their loving.
Happy together, they never spoke of children.

One day, in her thirtieth year, on the way to work,
her radio told her a baby boy—alive—
had been found in a dumpster, taken to hospital,
the mother was being sought.
                                      Then the wall gave way
in her memory; she was 15 years old again;
she swung the car, drove without conscious thought
to the hospital, cried to the nurse at the desk,
"They've found my baby—I thought he was dead, I'd never
have put him there alive..."
                                      The woman stared.
"He can't be yours. He's Asian and, besides,
the mother's found. The grandmother's come to get him.
That's her, over there, waiting her right to go."

She saw a dark-haired woman holding a bundle
wrapped in a shawl, and went to her, demanding:
"I have to see him." Silently the woman
opened the shawl. She saw the face, eyes open,
then the child puckered its mouth. Melita fainted.

"You should have told me—not borne this by yourself!"
Allen, his arms around her, knelt by the bed
they had put her in. She had told him everything—
it all came back: the force of a hard body

8

hurtling out of the bushes to fall upon her,
the hand smelling of urine pressed to her mouth,
the pain of the penetration, the staggering home,
the months of keeping her secret, afraid to tell,
then the child born dead. "And I was glad," she wept.

"You should have told me!"
                              "There was no way to tell you—
"It was all locked up in my head—I didn't remember."
He wiped away her tears. "We could have a child
of our own,..Would you like that?" "Yes," she said.

But after the nurse had sent him home she lay
awake and watched the searchlights from the roof
chalking a path along the wall, as once
she watched the moon. She stared at a grim future.
Now that her mind had let the rapist out
he would not go in again. She saw him always
faceless in a bedroom corner, waiting his chance
to have his turn at her. The baby, too,
would wait, mouth pursed as if to snatch a nipple.
It wasn't something Allen would understand.
Dawn was greying the room before she slept.

Only a year later their daughter was born,
a happy and healthy child, avid for life,
emptying both breasts at a single feeding.
"Now you have her," asked Allen, "can you forget
the other?
              She lifted her eyes to meet his squarely.
"What other? Our life's complete—there's just us three."

The joy that leaped in his face was worth the lie.

Rachel in Israel: January 1991

In a sealed room in the city of Tel Aviv
we who remember well the buzz-bombs of London
sit stiffly, waiting, in unpadded chairs.
We are older now. No war is easy.
Words sift slowly through gas masks, air enters thin.
We are aware it is a limited resource.

Young people also are here, bravado their
                            touchstone.
They jostle, joke, giggle,
exchange farcical kisses through gas masks.
Danger drives one's adrenalin. Oh, I remember
those nights of refuge in the Waterloo subway,
how cold and damp it was, and how comforting
to lie in a blanket in a neglected corner
in the arms of my carelessly chosen but adequate
                            lover,
sated with sex and wine, and no names exchanged—

That man must be dead now and the girl he
                            fathered
born in my mother's house on the morning of D-Day
is herself a mother, her son a schoolboy in Britain
who flies home tomorrow to answer the call of his
                            regiment,

And the man I was never able to bear a child for
who brought me long ago to live in our homeland
sits beside me now, his fingers closed over mine,
twisting the rings he gave me. And I think again
of my good grandson in London, so soon a soldier,
and pray that a girl lies curled in his arms this
                              moment—

For love is the true sealed room, the unfailing air.
I lean on my husband's shoulder, breathe hard.

Sabbath and Sandwiches

Tide's out
the pier deserted
fishermen here since dawn
have dumped their unused bait
into shallow water,
gone home with their catch.
The world's best-fed pelicans
heavy with harvest
doze on the railing.

On the sand below
a few yards closer to shore
some lesser-fed humans
lean in a row on the sea wall
near a cardtable
set by a church committee
with wrapped sandwiches
thermos jugs
and paper cups.

Food is not yet being served.
A young preacher
is unleashing a sermon.
He is not comfortable in his role.
His clean white shirt
already succumbing to heat
clings to his body as he gestures
his voice rises
gestures grow wider
he's giving it all he's got...

His audience, sticky in clothes
still stiff with yesterday's sweat,
grows restless. A newcomer asks his neighbor,

"How long must we listen to all these ravin's
before we get fed?"

His neighbor has been here before.
"Relax," he answers.
"He's winding down—
he'll get to the food in a jiffy.
Then we can eat. Food's good.
And you gotta remember
what it says somewhere in the Bible—
it's the ravin's that feed us."

For Lost and Luckless Lives

No monument
ever arose to honor
those dead good people
I still remember with pain—
some slain by poverty
and some by drink
others (women, mostly)
done in by love.

No stones reprise their names
their dust being long ago
strained through the gills of fishes,
settled to sea bottom.
They were lost
they were luckless
loved but to no avail;
in the grey of a bitter dawn
I build this cairn to their memory,

relive the ending of hope,
the weight of their pull
on my heartstrings,
and how grief squeezed this heart
like a sponge
when they chose to let go.

The Tenth Day of August

Too hot today
    the ocean can spare us no breezes
    electric fan's
    turned into a furnace
    coffee poured an hour ago
    still steams in the cup
    and I feel like an egg
    bounced wild in a boiling pot
    heat's got my yolk now—
    just heard it click solid!

    I'm done for—
    ladle me out!
    bless me with ice water
    peel off my skin—
    slice me with a chilled knife
    I want to die cold.

Two Views of One Suicide

At first the wound seemed trivial,
a stony word
flung from his mouth
slammed into the wall
of her heart
bruising the left ventricle
so she fell to her bed.

"It will heal."
doctors assured her,
and sent her a bottle of pills,
which she opened and set
by her waterglass—
she knew
her only cure was a poultice
of honeyed talk
from that same hard mouth.

But of course
those words never came—
and Laura's quite dead now.

IF

Daily we watched you
battle the rockstrewn path
to the door of his heart—
a door locked and bolted,
braced tight by the weight
of his will.

Your knocks and shy entreaties
came to us
tiny as bird cries
his silence boomed
in our ears

until last Saturday
when you couldn't come
and he, breaking loose the door,
lunged down that same hard path
crying your name.

So you won, I guess—
if death is a way of winning,
if, in that place you are now,
it counts
that he's sorry.

Curtain for Christy

We missed the first act,
having entered late,
without a program,
and bearing our own distractions
in rattling thought-bags.

When we first saw her
she was in center stage,
in full command
of her element,
emanating joy,
a small sure person
surrounded by light.

But the play moved onward.
Graciously she accepted
the scheduled darkening,
the measured encroachment
of shadow—
spotlights flickering,
dying, one by one,
till her space grew narrow
as a hospital bed
and serene in that slender radiance
she smiled and left us.

We felt the shock,
the velvet and absolute thud,
of the curtain falling,
we staggered with loss—
then rose in a standing ovation
to a bravura performance,
a classic adherence
to the demands of that one role
for which we all wait
in assigned rows
to audition.

The Dispersal of Immortal Remains

There was a poet once
whose wordsong rippled like water
through the course
of his springtime,

whose tongue struck fire from his teeth
when he uttered the name
of that woman whose flame
scorched his eyes
with the startle
of foxfire...

Poems came of their fusion,
not all of them written.

And where are they now?
He dead under a sea
roiled red with blood,
and she of the emerald eyes
rigid beneath an
alabaster cross,

and those glorious leftover words
he had never encapsuled
float gossamer as mothwings
through air into any room
where a poet, his own muse
throttled by love,
may marvel when they alight
and reassemble themselves
on his white empty page.

If you do not need a poem,
you should close your door now.

Juby

She was an ample woman
born near the turn of the century
product of the Texas rangelands—
of big-hearted people
who never read a novel
but lived them all
in one role or another—
daughter of a roundup camp cook
father unconfirmed...

As if to compensate for this lack
she acquired four husbands—
a cowpoke, two gamblers,
a traveling salesman,
all dead, their names forgotten;
she referred to them only by number:
"Number One gave me this,"
when she showed me a garnet brooch
or, "I got this suit
to wear to Number Four's funeral."

There were children, too,
scattered about the country,
loving children, she said,
though she saw them rarely.
There were grandchildren,
great-grandchildren
and a sprinkling of great-greats
They sent her letters and greeting cards
clothes she poked into her bulging closet
and never wore.

Her house was small
but her heart was big as a circus tent
open to all
neighbors, stray cats
young people in need of shelter
always she kept one corner for me.

We knew her as Juby—Juby Dawson—
last name courtesy of Number Four,
but when she turned 90 and decided
to return to Texas and live
with a widowed daughter,
I was the one she asked to help her pack,
and she took from under the oilcloth
lining of a dresser drawer
a yellowed paper.

"My baptism certificate," she told me...
"There's my birth date—July 9, 1904.
"No government records kept then—
at least not in Tinbucket, Texas.
But I showed this paper to the folks
at Social Security
and they gave me my pension
without batting an eye.

"Look," she said, "how my mama writ my name,
so pretty and clear though she only
went through sixth grade."
And I took the paper in my hand and read
what that longago unwed mother had written
in letters tall and proud after Name of Child:
"Jubilee Cornflower Rasmussen."

A Purpose in Life

Don't call this family dysfunctional.
It functioned smoothly,
more so than yours or mine,
ran purposefully,
steered by the cunning
of a sickened mind,
fueled by an anger
that never burned out,
time-set to destroy
the wife who fed him
and the children she bore.

The wife died without argument,
the children sullenly
accepted their sentence,
eroded quickly
into drugs and alcohol,
died early.
Their offspring fled
the mind dissolved
the family appeared to die out—

Great-grandchildren
in their scattered worlds
grew tall without knowing—
until that fateful hour
when it blossomed within them—
that they, too,
had been blessed with the legacy
and the need
to parcel out death.

Letting Go

How proud you are today,
how much aglow,
love like a bird live-taken
in your hand.
Listen and understand:
Open your fingers, so.
The joy of love
is in the letting go,
the spendor
when it does not fly away.

Responsibility

I am aware
it is an aberration of the eye
that renders the sky blue,
and that this view,
spreading before me
summer-gold and green,
is but a nerve end's lie
and if not seen
would not be beautiful
but dull
and uniformly gray...

So wise men say, and I
accepting this with equanimity
will put my work aside,
forget my chores,
and run outdoors
to stare and stare and stare
at everything,
any and everywhere,
fulfilling my responsibility
to make such beauty be.

After the Fairy Tale

Said the prince as he danced
with a girl he once knew,
"You're so sweet and so pleasant
I wish I'd wed you!
The wife Mother chose is
excessively grumpy,
and she won't share my bed—
says the mattress is lumpy."

His partner replied,
"Well, she's right, beyond doubt;
Your mother should toss
those old matteresses out!
I slept not a wink
when I stayed there one night,
but I just couldn't say so—
I'm much too polite!"

Counting the Silver

To succeed in politics
you must start young,
be born with a silver spoon
in your mouth
and a fork in your tongue,
and then acquire the knack
very early in life
for finding the exact place
in a rival's back
to drive home the knife.

Definition

Peace
is the pretty word
we call the recess
between the killing off
of one generation
and the growing tall
of the next.

A Day with Jonnie

On a day when my sensibilities
were ruffled, by small vexations,
like the neck of a partridge,

my wise daughter
carted me off to the mountains,
consigned me to an afternoon
of jays in silver pines,
chipmunks on oak trunks,
a bobtail cat for my lap
and a dog too big for that
who sat on my feet...

It was the home of
Marge and Jimmy
two happy people
who coddled me with kindness
cajoled me with cinnamon coffee
and when the dark came
lent me the eye of their telescope
to spy on Jupiter
and his concubine moons...

Returned to the city
by my wise daughter
I fell gratefully into bed,
golden moons dancing on eyelids,
feathers so smooth
a hurricane could not disturb them.

All the Way Home

It was not that the child was small
or the mother so stricken
when he pried the grey bundle
from her to bury it

nor that the grave must be narrow
the war that had brought him here
having fathered a field of mounds
from him to horizon—
no, it was the small foot
that fell from its wrappings
as he slid her down,
reminding him of the daughter
whose foot he had fondled
only a week ago,
counting each toe as a pig
in the nursery rhyme;

it was the way these other toes
seemed to curl in his hand
as he pushed them back
under the blanket
that wrenched from him sobs
and tears that blinded his eyes
to the work of his shovel
that must dig until sundown.

He came home at last,
but nothing is quite the same,
though his job was waiting,
and his wife patient,
and his blue-eyed daughter
still loves her daddy
even if he always refuses
to count any piggies.

31

Duel at Sunset

One day I saw a man and kite in combat,
The kite had the shape of a fish,
tugged at the string
like a marlin fighting a line.
and the man below—
an old man, bent of shoulder
and limping some—
played it as if it were.
He paid out line,
and the kite ran with it;
he wrapped line over his wrist
and brought it low...

But the kite had its own devices,
rose on a wave of wind
so high, so strong,
the man stumbled and fell
(he got up laughing).
White in a reddening sky
the kite defied him,
cavorted gently, waiting
what chance might come.

I watched till the sun
slid into sea,
then had to go—
I had to leave them at it;
but carry the memory with me
like a found treasure
to fondle in my mind,
though I cannot begin
to guess who was playing whom
or who was at last reeled in.

Writing Class, With Distractions

The garden of Small is too big for an eye
to see with a series of secretive glances.
The class is in session and reading and I
should be giving some heed but a butterfly dances
among the azaleas, and ribbons of sun
are strung like a maypole from low-bending trees
and a wisp of a web that a spider has spun
still wet from the morning dries out in the breeze.
The mystery writer is taking her turn,
the story is gory with intricate plot,
but a bird's at the window. If I never learn
who murdered the lady and how he was got,
it's the fault of the garden of Emmett Small,
and I'm not to be blamed at all.

Timberline

Sickles of wind are slashing the alder branches,
but the trail to the summit runs carelessly,
mile after mile,
knowing a wind that is lord in this valley of ranches
will find in a little while
its strength shaken and affronted—
held at the timberline
where the edge of its steel will be blunted
on pine and higher-than-pine...

on red trees heavy with centuries, not shaking
under the knifed onslaught, a stout hedge
resisting the valley wind till it falls back, quaking,
from the clean-whipped ledge....

Silence piles thicker than snow on that mountainside
where a wind has died.

Taming the Wild One

Melanie is tearful—that wild poet
she tamed with satin sheets
and her dad's wine cellar
has gone over the fence
with no formal goodbye,
is even now yodeling
beneath the inferior balcony
of an uglier girl.

Oh, Melanie, Melanie,
you should have called me
before you started this project!
I could have told you the poet
can never be tamed—
is of the cat family,
will slip any collar,
never enters a situation
before he has sniffed out an exit.

Yet, left in his feral state,
he can love you truly—
does not need sheets at all,
will bring his own bottle,
nurse you through illness,
scatter your name in his poems,
even dedicate books to you;

and, being vegetarian,
can be fed cheaply.

When he comes back, Melanie,
be enigmatic in welcome;
tell him Dad locked up the cellar,
the sheets have been lost by the laundry,
and you feel your life is taking a new direction;
you have tried hang-gliding,
signed for a class in karate—

Look deep into his lion-eyes
as you say all this;
the bait he can never resist
is the chance to tame you!

Night Burial

(For a Mexican girl, burned in a house fire,
buried after sundown so field workers could attend.)

The sacramental stars are lit
above the grave where Lupe lies,
sweet desert blossoms cover it,
and mockingbirds with muted cries
remind us what is mortal dies,
returns to earth from which it sprung,
an ending no one old denies,
but she was beautiful and young.
And so for her sad songs are sung,
for her white stars burn in the sky,
and words well meant to tell us why
fall graceless from a troubled tongue.

Unreined

We saw her seldom
she came out only on mornings
when her inner tempest propelled her
then we watched in wonder
as she mounted her whirlwind
and bareback and bridleless
rode full gallop
to the very brink of horizon.

The day she was thrown
we ran to lift her body
it was lifeless
all spirit gone
and nothing in her face
to tell us why
she rode her pain so hard
or who it was
had taken the bridle from her.

A Twig in the Process of Bending

I pick at random one picture out of scores.
The townfolk of Douglas, Alaska, 1914,
honor the summer solstice, eat outdoors,
line up for pictures against the pervading green,
women in white from parasol to toe,
well-bearded men like Father in the front row.

But Mother and I are missing—I wonder why.
A magnifying glass in time discerns,
screened from the crowd but caught by the camera's eye,
a woman tending a child which as it turns
lets garment down with obvious intention—
my first recorded flouting of convention!

Marcellena

Her god was generic,
she had no use for the brand names
they sold him under
in local churches and temples,
places she entered only
when a wedding or burial
demanded her presence.

She took her people straight, too.
One look at black-headed Charlie
and that was it.
Both families deplored the union,
but they married young
and lived together
happy though childless
for forty years.

When Charlie died a neighbor
bearing condolence and curiosity
in equal portions
asked her, "Your husband—
was he Oriental?"
She answered, "I never noticed"
and seemed surprised at the question.

Marcellena died forthrightly
as she lived
one day vigorous, washing windows,
the next stretched lifeless
on the kitchen floor.

There was nothing unique
in the contents of the cardboard box
we emptied into the ocean a week ago.
Her ashes shared a wave
with a governor's lady.
She would not have been flattered;
she believed in the sameness of all.

She was black—but she never noticed.

Breaking Through

On a gunny sack beside the fire
our beagle worries a bone.
Hard and dry, it nimbly
slips from the menace of teeth,
but he makes a vise of his paws
and growls his intention
to splinter that ivory
or else!

At the kitchen table
I worry a stubborn poem,
turn a phrase sideways,
backward and upside down,
adjust the meter,
toss out the empty rhyme,
hellbent to loose
from that encapsuled thought
the juice of real meaning.

Crack! Bang!
The crack is the bone succumbing,
the bang the dog's tail
thumping the floor
in salute of victory.
His head lifts, eyes gleam,
the rich marrow he craved
drips from his tongue.

Well done, beagle!
I at my littered table
may gnaw until breakfast.

Impostor

Her calm is legend—
except at the symphony,
when she slides into music naked
as into water,
leaving the thoughts that clothed her
piled high on the green bank of forgetfulness;
then, as an otter
plays in a waterfall,
gives herself to the plunge,
a torrent of sound,
that sweeps her into its maelstrom,
down, down, until only
her pale hair floats on the surface;

and she might well drown there
except the conductor saves her,
his lowered baton
abruptly impounding the flow
strands her on an island of silence,
grace notes dripping like sequins
from her bruised thighs....

And still there is time
while applause shatters the air
to wrap herself once more
in indifference,
time even to replace,
before the lights go on
and we look at her,
that quite unreadable face.

In Defense

Taking little notice of
her womanly ambitions
he captured her with words of love
and all of the positions,
explored her beauty bodily
from lip to breast to bottom,
but left her mind a mystery,
and that is why she shot him!

In the Memory Store

"We buy your memories"—that's what the sign said,
and Jericho, whose right to run the store
came through inheritance, first smiled at it,
then found it fitting. Each item to be sold
—flat iron or butter churn or phonograph—
had once belonged to someone and would go
to someone else in whose mind a memory
triggered its purchase.

                    He dusted up a little,
polished the windows, waxed the once-painted floors,
accepted the back-room quarters as his own,
and when a year had passed and customers
once loyal to Aunt Lou now trusted him,
because his heart still spoke a southern accent,
bought a magnolia tree and planted it
beside his bedroom window. He named it Scarlett.

Late in the second year his clientele
expanded strangely when people who had no home,
seeking a place where being shelterless
need not mean freezing, came to San Diego.
Some of them found his store. He ended buying
watches and rings and wallets he did not want
and couldn't sell. He wouldn't buy their shoes
or other things they needed, but gave them money
and maybe a cup of coffee, and waved them on.
"There, but for Aunt Lou's kindness, might go I,"
he told himself, and paid the next one double.

One night a man came just before closing time
and said abruptly, "I want to sell a memory."

Jericho cursed that sign. "I'm not a writer."
"Listen, a twenty'd do me. This story's worth it.
Besides, I need to tell it." Jericho saw
the need was evident. "I guess I could give you ten—
and you could still sell your story to a writer
in case you find one. Sit in that chair. I'll listen."

An hour later, having experienced hell in Vietnam
for sixty minutes, he silently pushed a twenty
into the pocket of the man whose hands
were pressed against his face. "I'll make some coffee."
His visitor shook his mane. "They dole out beds
at the Salvation Army—there'll be a line there.
Thanks for the money—and for listening."
"Thank you for telling me." He couldn't say
with all his heart he wished he had not heard it.

That was the start of a bizarre procession
of people selling memories; the first one
must have told others; each one came alone,
each with a story chilling to the blood,
each with a need to tell it.

                              His funds vanished.
In desperation, he cut what he paid in half,
then to five dollars; still the sellers came.
One night he took the sign down; the next morning
fearing he might fail someone, he put it back.

The trouble was, the memories wouldn't go.
He didn't expect the ones who sold them to him
to cart them off again; still, he was not prepared
to hear their voices, heavy and humorless,
coming from walls he counted on for quiet.

One memory seemed inhabiting a vase,
another filled the thumb of a baseball mitt,
and all of them seemed settled in forever.
He plugged an old radio in to drown them out.

One thing encouraged him—no women came.
He feared their memories more than the ones of war!
But then a woman did come, out of the rain,
stood for a moment dripping at the doorway,
left sandals on the mat and walked barefooted
to where the chess set stood on a marble table.

"That's not for sale," he said (though he liked her legs).
"It's all I took from my old life into this one."
"I know. I've passed here often and seen you playing,
you against you. I thought you might play me.
I'm not too awful at it. My dad taught me.
My name is Clancy."
                    "Clancy, just take that chair!"
He won the first game easily. The next
was hers. "You're good, you know," he told her.
"I'm glad you didn't add 'for being a woman.'"
She rose. "I've got to go."
                    "Just one more game?"
"I can't. They hold a bed for me at the 'Y'
but only if I'm there by eight."
                    "Come back, then."
"I'll try." He went to hold the door for her,
watched her lithe body til dark swallowed it,
drank in the rain, cold and ambiguous,
"I should have kept her. Not likely she'll be back."

But she came back and soon it was a given
she would arrive at six and share his salad

and sandwiches, leave only to claim her bed;
until one night the cold rain came again,
and he, made bold by pure desire, said, "Stay."

"I always wanted to," she said, and did.

Clancy changed everything, and every change
was to his liking, especially when he found
those memories needed dust to feed upon
and once she finished dusting all were gone.
Clancy cooked meals, too; no more sandwiches,
but soups and casseroles and home-made bread.
She planned a garden for the early spring,
trimmed Scarlett's branches when they scraped the window,
mended his clothes, mended his life as well.

The best thing was, she had no memories
to sell; the ones she shared were happy days
of tomboy childhood in the middle west,
an early marriage dissolved without a hurt
to anyone; a job in an auto plant
that moved to Mexico; even her tales
of poverty and homelessness were funny.
"How did you happen to come to San Diego?"
he asked her, knowing well his own heart's hunger
had dragged her from the corn belt. When she answered,
"Somehow I felt I should," he knew a prayer
he never made had somehow found an answer.

She never asked about his past existence.
He did not tell her, swore he never would,
although he often felt her eyes upon him,
reading his face as if to find a reason
to make some sense of why they were together.

One night when a full moon fell like heavy snow
across their bed, she startled him by saying,
"I know one thing about you, Jericho.
You were a priest once."

                              "Well, I tried to be.
How did you guess?"

                              "The way you put your hands
on people's heads after they tell their sorrows,
as if you bless them—and I think you do."
She rolled her body over him, kissed his mouth.
"With this kiss, Jericho, I buy your memory."

And then the hurts he never thought to share
broke into words; he told her all that happened,
when God went one way and his church another,
and neither found a niche to fit him into.
He talked the moon to dark, the night to gray
of early dawn and when it all was told
she whose hot tears had wet his chest said only,
"Your ministry is here, I'll help you with it,
Sleep now—"
                    "I love you, Clancy."

                              "Yes, I know.
Now sleep—the past is gone now, Jericho."

He slept and woke at last to see her standing
beside the bedroom door, brushing her hair
in an aureole of sun.

                    "I guess Rhett Butler
gave a damn after all," she told him laughing.
"I just looked out the window. Scarlett's in bud!"

A Reason for Pebbles

If it were possible, always,
forever, to walk
by the bedrail fence
and the field where the mower has been,
at the time of the day
when the cattle are coming in,
and the shadows even of rabbits
are suddenly high,
and the blue dusk darkens the sky,
we would never have need for talk.
The wings of our might-have-been words
would be folded like sleeping birds,
your handclasp would speak to me.
Love would just be.

But fences come to an end
and the day is drowned
in the colder dusk and the sound
of aircraft drones in our ears
loud as the bawling of steers.
Soon miles, then days, will divide us.

And that is the reason I choose,
while the silence still is between us,
a feather that happened to fall
from a hawk that was circling around,
or a yellow leaf from the ground,
or any old pebble at all,
just something to carry away
to touch, to remind me of—
in the din of a difficult day—
a place and a face that I love.

In Alexandria

In Alexandria where the books were burned
sending their shrieks of smoke into the sky
words still lie smoldering and refuse to die
and sting the air whenever soil is turned:

Those kings are dead who loved the compelling word,
the generals gone, who fed the books to flame,
and still the cries of some forgotten name
reproach us for the songs we never heard.

Whenever

If I should die tomorrow, and these hands
that answered always answer not again
the cry of bud and root, if for the pain
in aging bone a quiet come instead,
and body do no more what life demands—

For all the love and joy and beauty lost,
great peace may come. I know too well the cost
of life to haggle over long with death,
having paid ardently in ache for breath
breathed upon mountains, and for careless joy
worn many a sackcloth.

                Could the mind employ
the engine of the heart to do its will
forever, and the body be forever
an instrument of love, and death be never,

I might relive old joys. But now against
the arm of time, irrevocably fenced
from life unending, I will take my leave,
divest my spirit of its body, trust
the nearest ocean to disperse my dust,
and, grateful for what life gave, commend my soul
to new dimensions, making wisdom whole.

For the Holy Season

Now is the holy season of the heart,
the homing time
when arms lift to embrace,
and love in illumined letters
inscribes the face,
and eyes burn candles
to guide the traveler in.

What life has taken
memory now restores.
Old hurts are laid to rest,
new dreams released;
and pilgrims seeking paradise
in actions foolish
oftener than wise,
and wounded fugitives
from private wars,
all, all, are welcome
at our feast!

Along time's chill
and ominous corridors
the light of loving
leaps from our opening doors,
as we pray together for peace,
for all the world's people,
peace!